A **NOVA**BOOK

Peak Performance

Sports, Science, and the Body in Action

Emily Isberg

Simon and Schuster Books for Young Readers
Published by Simon & Schuster Inc., New York

In association with WGBH Boston,
producers of NOVA for public television

SIMON AND SCHUSTER
BOOKS FOR YOUNG READERS
Simon & Schuster Building
Rockefeller Center
1230 Avenue of the Americas
New York, NY 10020

Manufactured in Spain.

10 9 8 7 6 5 4 3 2 1
10 9 8 7 6 5 4 3 2 1 (pbk.)

Library of Congress
Cataloging-in-Publication Data
Isberg, Emily.
    Peak performance: sports, science,
and the body in action / Emily Isberg.
    (A NOVABOOK)
    "In association with WGBH Boston,
producers of NOVA for public television."
    Includes index.
    Summary: Describes the ways in
which scientific advances have contrib-
uted to athletic performance focusing on
sports medicine and the work of the U.S.
Olympic Training Centers.
    1. Sports sciences–Juvenile litera-
ture. 2. Physical education and
training–Juvenile literature. 3. Performance – Juvenile literature. [1. Sports
sciences. 2. Physical education and
training.] I. WGBH (Television station :
Boston, Mass.) II. NOVA (Television
program) III. Title. IV. Series.
GV558.I82 1989
796–dc19
89-30063 CIP AC

ISBN 0-671-67750-0
ISBN 0-671-67747-0 (pbk.)

This book is dedicated to Marc,
Matthew, Elizabeth, and Rachel.

I would like to thank Gail Conway, Siri Larsen and Michael
Stott and their families, and
Glenn Tremml for so willingly
sharing their triumphs and
adversities. I am also indebted
to Leonard Jansen, Peter Van
Handel, and the many helpful
people at the U.S.O.C. Sports
Science Program, and to Dr.
Arthur Pappas of University of
Massachusetts Medical Center
for his invaluable suggestions.
    Special thanks go to the ath-
letes, coaches, scientists, and
physicians who generously
shared their time and expertise.
Among those not named in the
text are Robert Axtell, Southern
Connecticut State University;
Sharon Gilligan, R.N., Julie
Powers, and Dr. John Warner,
Children's Hospital Medical
Center; Norman Heglund,
Harvard University; Kathleen
Helsing, Massachusetts Depart-
ment of Public Health; Jim
McKay, Dartmouth Physical Ther-
apy; SportsMedicine Systems,
Inc.; Wayne Wescott, YMCA;
and Dr. Bert Zarins, New Eng-
land Patriots.
    I also wish to thank Nancy
Lattanzio, Gaye Korbet, Elise
Katz, Susan Spellman, Matthew
Bartholomew, M J Walsh and
Paula Apsell, executive producer
of NOVA for making this project
possible.

The NOVA television series is
produced by WGBH Boston.
Funding for the series is provided
by public television stations, the
Johnson & Johnson Family of
Companies, and Lockheed
Corporation.

**The 100-meter backstroke
(title page) and the 100-
meter sprint (right) at the
1988 Summer Olympic
Games: two tests of the
human urge to push per-
formance to the limit.**

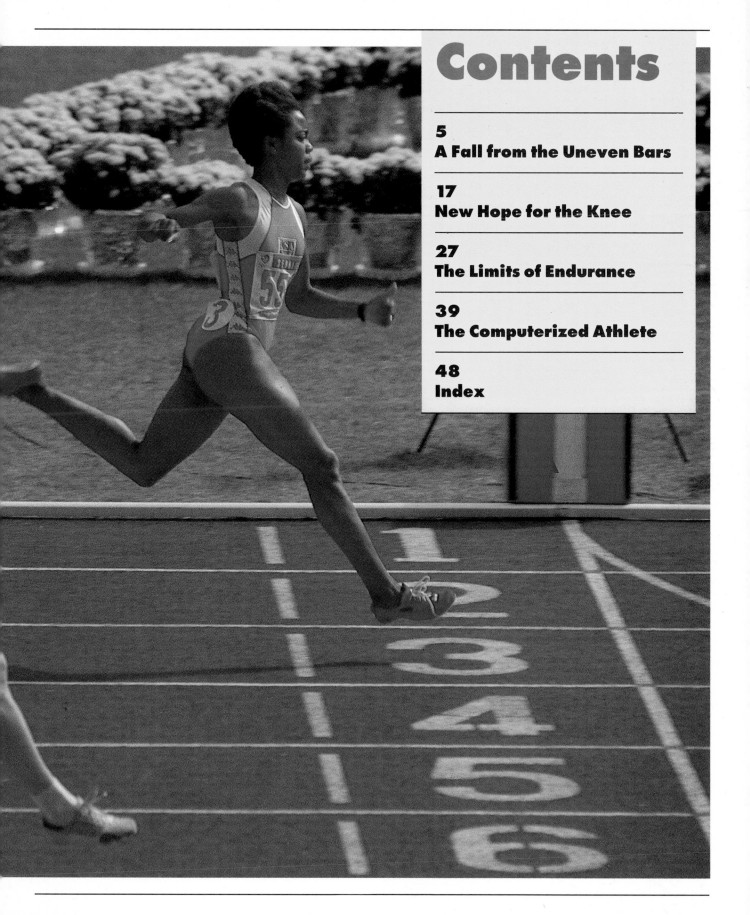

Contents

5
A Fall from the Uneven Bars

17
New Hope for the Knee

27
The Limits of Endurance

39
The Computerized Athlete

48
Index

A Fall from the Uneven Bars

Twelve-year-old Siri Larsen has been training for six years for moments like this. Hundreds of people in an exhibition hall in Oslo, Norway, are holding their breaths to see what she will do next. Her competitors, gymnasts from all over northern Europe, size her up with envy. The young gymnast from Massachusetts composes herself, bolts down the runway, bounds from the vaulting board in a straddle split that takes her over the low bar up to the high bar, and launches into her routine.

The lightning-fast moves build to a climax. From a handstand on the high bar, Siri will swing down and up again, let go for a front flip high in the air, and catch the bar on the way back down. Only this time she misses. She falls to the ground with her arms outstretched, fracturing and dislocating her elbow.

"I was in shock," says Siri. "My arm felt weird, tingly. I yelled for my coach, Bob, and burst out crying."

Siri will get emergency treatment in Oslo. Then she will fly home to visit her own doctor, who specializes in sports medicine. Not long ago, an injury like this could have shattered her dreams of one day competing in the Olympics. But today, the steps her doctor recommends help her return fully and quickly to her sport.

Although she had never visited a university lab or been the subject of an experiment, this was not the first time Siri had benefited from sports science. Research in fields from psychology and nutrition to computer science and engineering has been quietly changing the way athletes like Siri train and equip themselves.

For gymnastics, engineers are designing new equipment that reduces the punishment an athlete's body must take. Biomechanists, using high-speed cameras and computers, are identifying safer, more efficient ways to perform high-level skills. Psychologists are helping athletes deal with the stress of competition, and coaches are using information on heart rate, respiration, and sleep to pace training programs so that athletes reach their peak without "overtraining" – suffering injury or fatigue before the contest even starts.

Opposite: Siri Larsen, twelve, sports the uniform of Norway's national gymnastics team.

Siri hurt her elbow attempting the "Jäger" (below), in which the gymnast starts from a handstand, swings around the high bar and up into a somersault in the air, then catches the bar on the way down.

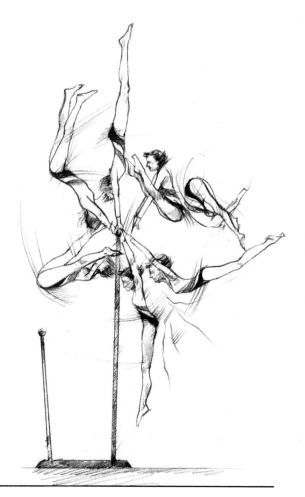

Equipped for Success

Unlike the football or hockey player, the gymnast wears no padding to protect herself from falls or impacts. Swinging eight feet (2.5 m) above the ground or hurdling into a vault, she has little margin for error. While learning new skills, the gymnast has traditionally relied on the coach to "spot," or catch her if she falls. Now there are alternatives: softer, thicker crash mats made of foam rather than horsehair; safety harnesses attached to the ceiling by rope; and perhaps most effective of all, safety pits, four- to eight-foot (1.2-2.5-m) deep holes filled with large blocks of urethane foam.

Gymnasts used to perform on bare wooden floors. Now these floors may have springs underneath to help kick the athlete into the air and a foam pad and carpet on the top to cushion her when she lands. The uneven parallel bars are now made of flexible fiberglass or graphite instead of wood, offering the gymnast a small boost, an extra fraction of a second to add a pike to a double back somersault as she dismounts. These improvements in equipment are enabling gymnasts to perform skills that were nearly impossible years ago.

Sports science is one of many tools athletes use as they push themselves to do what no one has done before. The results can be spectacular. "Women's gymnastics has changed completely in the last fifteen, twenty years," says Bob Colarossi, Siri's coach at the Massachusetts Gymnastics Center. "What Olga Korbut did to win the Olympic gold medal in 1972 wouldn't win a state championship at the lowest level today. What Nadia Comaneci did in '76 – she mounted onto the floor with a double full twist – is not even an elite-level skill anymore. The 'easiest' elite tumbling pass is now harder than that."

Not everyone is satisfied with the direction that sports science is taking. Some feel that too much emphasis is placed on winning. They fear that technology has helped increase the level of competition to the point that too much is demanded of young, growing bodies; and that to satisfy these demands, athletes in many sports have turned to steroids and other drugs that are believed to enhance performance but have dangerous side effects. Other people feel that scientific research can play a positive role in making athletics safe and in helping people like Siri excel.

This book does not recommend or endorse the medical treatments or training regimens described in its pages, or tell you how to get in shape. Instead, it is a sampler, offering a taste of new ideas in several sports-related fields and a look at how exercise can change the human body. Even if you don't want to do a handspring on the balance beam or run a two-hour marathon, understanding the body in action can help you appreciate the accomplishments of those who do – and make the most of your own efforts, whatever level you seek to achieve.

And it can help you appreciate how Siri Larsen got back on the uneven bars.

Today's flexible bars give an extra boost to gymnasts like Olympic bronze-medalist Phoebe Mills, fifteen.

Like a Cat in the Air

Siri grew up with a U.S. family, but was born in Cambodia during the last months of the Vietnam War. Two relief workers found her abandoned by the roadside. Weighing scarcely more than two pounds (1 kg), she was so small they fed her with an eyedropper.

Siri was born with an aptitude for gymnastics, says Bob Colarossi. "She's like a cat in the air," he explains. "Many students become confused when they turn upside down . . . . and try to put their feet down against empty space. But when Siri's in the air, she knows exactly where the ground is. She always lands on her feet." Siri also has an incredible visual memory. She can watch other gymnasts perform complicated routines and then do them herself.

Siri is an "elite" athlete, the highest level a gymnast can attain. At the age of eleven, she was invited by Norway, the country where her adoptive father grew up, to join its national gymnastics team. Now, when she's not competing, she's training. The elite gymnast must master hundreds of skills in four events: floor exercises (tumbling), uneven parallel bars, balance beam, and vault. In the weeks before a meet, Siri works out four hours a day after school, plus two hours before school. On Saturdays she's back at the gym from 8 A.M. until noon. There's not much time for anything but gymnastics. "I go to school, go to the gym, do my homework, and go to bed," she says about a typical day. "It's hard work, but it's fun, too."

Competing as an elite athlete demands as much as six hours a day in the gym, but Siri still has time for a laugh.

Siri's routine on the four-inch-wide (10-cm) beam includes handsprings and a dismount with a double back somersault.

The Elbow

The elbow is particularly important to gymnasts because, unlike most of us, they walk, cartwheel, balance, and support themselves on their hands. As a hinge joint, the elbow allows the arm to bend. But this versatile joint can also twist, allowing you to turn your hand enough to open the door, write your name, and tie your shoe.

Three bones come together at the elbow: the *ulna* and the *radius* (forearm bones) and the *humerus* (upper arm bone). The *biceps* and *triceps* muscles work together to move the elbow as a hinge. When the biceps muscle contracts, it pulls the radius closer to the shoulder, raising and flexing the arm. Muscles can pull but not push. The triceps muscle must contract to pull the arm straight.

Three types of connective tissue help the elbow joint work: *tendons*, which attach muscles to bones and protect them from shock; *ligaments*, cords that hold the bones together and allow the joint to bend, but not in the wrong directions; and *cartilage*, a material three times as slippery as ice that helps the bones slip past each other without grinding.

Split-Second Fall, Ten-Week Recovery

Siri's fall from the uneven bars occurred on October 29, 1987, at the beginning of a five-week trip to competitions in Europe. X rays showed that she had suffered a minor "avulsion fracture." One of the elbow ligaments, the ropelike cords that hold together the joint, had torn free of its moorings, carrying with it a tiny piece of the bone in her forearm. In addition, one of her lower arm bones (the *ulna*) had popped out of the joint, damaging the tissues around it. The Norwegian doctor put the bone back in place, put her arm in a large plaster cast, and told her to keep it on for a month.

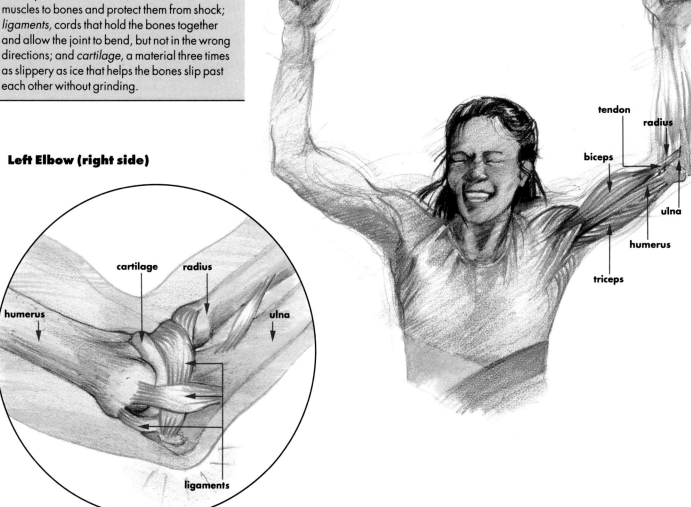

Left Elbow (right side)

Dejectedly, Siri flew back home. A few days later, she visited her own physician, Dr. Frank Bunch, Jr., at a sports medicine clinic. Dr. Bunch is an orthopedic surgeon, a specialist in problems of the skeleton. He was concerned that if he left the cast on the full four weeks, Siri might lose some of the range of motion in her elbow. Mobility is especially important to the gymnast, who needs her joints to be in top-notch shape to perform high-level skills.

"You want to get the joint moving as soon as you can safely," explains Dr. Bunch. Otherwise, the ligaments can tighten up permanently. The muscles start to waste away, not only from the injury but also from lack of use. Dr. Bunch put a removable splint on Siri's forearm so she could take it off to do rehabilitation exercises, beginning that very day.

Siri worked hard at recovering. To stay in shape, she conditioned with her team and practiced skills, like cartwheels, that she could do with only one arm. She went to physical therapy three times a week. At first, she did "elbow crankers" with her injured arm – flexing and straightening the joint as much as she could without causing further damage – warming the tissues up first in a whirlpool bath so they would stretch, and icing them down afterward so they wouldn't swell.

After six weeks, Siri could straighten her arm almost the whole way. She began working out on a Cybex machine, one of a new generation of exercise machines that physical therapists use to identify and strengthen weak muscles. Siri used the Cybex to strengthen the biceps, the triceps, and the other major muscle groups that move the elbow. Her arm was strapped to a lever that moved at a steady rate set by her physical therapist. As the lever moved, she pushed it as hard as she could. If she felt pain and eased up, the resistance would decrease automatically. When an athlete lifts weights the resistance is determined by the number of pounds she stacks onto the bar. But when Siri used the Cybex, the resistance was determined by how hard she pushed.

As well as exercise, the machine also provided a sensitive measurement of Siri's muscle strength. When her left arm was 95 percent as strong as her right, Dr. Bunch said she could gradually resume work on her routines, at first taping her elbow for support.

Boston Red Sox pitcher Roger Clemens works out on a Cybex machine to condition his pitching arm. The Cybex is one of a new generation of exercise machines that can be used to identify and strengthen weak muscles. It also provides sensitive measurements of strength that can help doctors and physical therapists monitor a patient's recovery. Siri used a Cybex until her injured left arm was 95 percent as strong as her right. Then she was able to resume work on her routines.

Kids and Sports Injuries
A sampling of 11 sports

Sport	Total injuries to all ages	Total injuries to kids ages 5 to 14	Percent of injuries to kids in each sport
Bicycling	574,098	334,575	58%
Football	329,987	124,458	38%
Playground	197,641	122,553	62%
Baseball	348,539	106,111	30%
Basketball	467,160	104,137	22%
Soccer	86,409	35,922	42%
Gymnastics	**34,217**	**21,517**	**63%**
Wrestling	35,585	12,490	35%
Track & Field	58,597	9,551	16%
Martial Arts	19,197	5,433	28%
Ice Hockey	17,698	3,451	20%

In 1987, sports-related injuries sent more than 1.25 million kids to hospital emergency rooms for treatment. * This chart shows the number of injuries that year in eleven major activities to all ages (including adults) and to kids ages five to fourteen. It also shows what percent of all injuries in these sports happened to kids. The activity with the most injuries for this age group was bicycle riding, followed by football, games using playground equipment, baseball and basketball. Kids' injuries account for roughly one-third of all sports-related injuries to all ages, but the percent varies for individual sports. Although gymnastics results in relatively few injuries overall, of these, nearly two-thirds are to kids. (Approximately 370,000 additional injuries were suffered by kids in other sports, not listed here.)

*These are injuries treated in emergency rooms only. At least twice as many are seen in doctor's offices.

Source: Consumer Product Safety Commission

Siri returned to competition after only ten weeks. "Normally, I'd tell patients they wouldn't be doing gymnastics for four months, much less competing," said Dr. Bunch. "But Siri worked hard and had good guidance from her coach and physical therapist. They made sure she didn't push herself too hard and cause damage to her elbow."

Training the Body

Gymnastics has been called "the football of girls' sports" because it has a relatively high risk of injury. Despite efforts to make the sport safer, says Bill Sands, director of sports science for the U.S. women's national gymnastics team, "injury is our major problem." The most accomplished athletes, attempting the most difficult maneuvers, face the greatest risk. To perfect a skill, the gymnast must repeat it hundreds of times. But repetitive stress on a single part of the body can lead to "overuse" injuries, like stress fractures or spondylolysis, a crack in the lower spine. A second type of injury can result from a single impact or accident, like Siri's fall from the uneven bars.

Not all injuries can be prevented. But many can be, says Bob Colarossi, through a carefully planned training program that includes warming up, stretching, and "conditioning," or strengthening exercises; state-of-the-art equipment; and learning skills in the proper sequence.

Siri and her teammates, the Masstars, begin their four-hour daily practice with fifteen minutes of jogging and calisthenics. The exercise sends blood flowing to their muscles and makes them warmer, looser, and less likely to tear under stress.

Stretching follows, with each stretch done slowly and held for several seconds. Stretching helps counteract the damaging effects of exercise, which can create small tears in muscle fibers. As a muscle heals, it becomes slightly shorter, like a piece of rope that has been ripped and stitched together. Stretching restores length to muscles. It also restores flexibility to joints, which is especially important for teenagers before and during a growth spurt.

"Strong, flexible bodies resist injury," says Colarossi. "Weak, tight bodies break." Gymnasts need exceptionally strong muscles to hold their bodies steady as they fly through the air, and to help their joints withstand the impact of so much running and jumping. Strength training, and weight training in particular, are receiving more attention in gymnastics and many other sports, especially as women pursue activities once reserved for men.

Colarossi does not use weights with his team, but he does lead them through a rigorous daily thirty-minute conditioning program. The gymnasts work and rest different parts of their bodies on alternate days. The program emphasizes the coordination and speed a gymnast needs to do maneuvers as demanding as performing three tricks in a three-second vault routine. On a typical day, Siri might run sprints, do five timed rope climbs using only her arms, and perform three sets of a dozen leg lifts while she hangs from a bar, done at the exhausting speed of fifteen seconds per set.

Siri needs strong arms and a little help from her coach for a handstand on the uneven bars.

After eight weeks of rehab, Siri went back to her routines with her elbow taped for support. By carefully exercising her injured elbow instead of keeping it immobile, she hastened her return to her sport.

Muscle Bound

To jump higher, members of the U.S. Olympic volleyball team built up the muscles in their arms. To run faster, 1988 Olympic superstar Florence Griffith-Joyner lifted weights. Swimmer Janet Evans, who at age seventeen won three gold medals at the same Olympic Games, pumped iron too.

In sports from running to baseball, athletes are discovering that from strength flows not only power but also speed and muscular endurance. Whether you use hand-held dumbbells or sophisticated exercise machines, all weight training techniques work the same way. They pit your muscles against resistance. Strength is built as you increase the resistance, a concept called "progressive overload."

Repeated stress thickens the fibers that make up muscles by increasing protein build-up. The thicker the muscle fibers, the stronger the contraction they can produce. The male sex hormone testosterone plays a role in making muscles bigger. That's why males don't bulk up until after puberty.

There are as many different ideas about how to weight train as there are coaches and trainers. A basic strength-training session includes exercises for all the major muscle groups, in sets of eight to twelve repetitions and using a weight heavy enough so that only twelve repetitions can be done. To develop explosive strength, some coaches use power lifting, in which the athlete does the lift only once with the maximum weight he can lift. Others have athletes develop muscular endurance by repeating the same exercise many times with a relatively light weight. Whatever the approach, weight training should be done only three times a week. Muscle fibers tear slightly during exercise, and need rest to rebuild themselves.

To improve performance, the athlete must do exercises that are "sport-specific," mimicking as closely as possible the movements used in competition. Siri does leg lifts to develop strength for maneuvers like the giant swing. In this skill, she falls forward from a handstand on the high bar, swings around the bar, and kicks her legs up into another handstand.

According to Sands, conditioning can help athletes most through "periodization," an approach that divides the year into "cycles" with different goals. In the first cycle, for example, when she is mastering new skills, the gymnast works on building a foundation of overall strength. Later, when she is weaving skills together into routines, she may spend less time on strength training but work at a higher intensity, focusing on sport-specific exercises.

To make sure athletes aren't training too hard, Sands monitors their heartrate and weight, and asks about their sleep patterns, illnesses, and feelings of fatigue. A computer program picks up any sudden changes. Overtraining, he says, is one of the worst things that can happen to an athlete. But the line between under- and overtraining is slim. The only way an elite gymnast can master all her skills is through practice, and more practice. She dare not venture into competition, away from the safety of foam pits, crash mats, and spotters until her routines are virtually automatic.

Champion swimmer Matt Biondi worked out in the weight room as well as the pool in his quest for Olympic gold. In sports from swimming to sprinting, athletes are pumping iron to get faster and stronger.

Preparing the Mind

When training for a meet, Siri and her teammates sometimes start their practice by lying down on the mat, closing their eyes, relaxing their bodies, and taking a few deep breaths. For the next half hour, the training is mental rather than physical, although the two are intertwined. Under the direction of psychologist Joseph Massimo, they will concentrate on a routine – for example, a performance on the four-inch-wide (10-cm), four-foot-high (1.2-m) balance beam – and mentally rehearse every move.

Siri imagines herself walking to the beam, nodding to the judge, and preparing to mount. She then springs from the board onto the beam and feels the narrow strip of padding under her feet. As she runs through the performance in her mind, she tenses the various muscle groups required to do her routine, from the first handspring to a perfect dismount – a double back somersault. She feels confident she can complete the routine without a hitch.

Mental rehearsal, also called "visualization," is used in one form or another by most top-ranking athletes today, says Massimo, who also is a gymnastics coach. It can even be used in team sports, helping a player to plan strategy and anticipate opponents' moves so she is not surprised during the game.

Psychologist Leonard Zaichkowsky, a consultant to the U.S. Olympic Committee, tells hockey players to involve all their senses in mental rehearsal. "When you see yourself making a body check, you should hear your skates crunching on the ice, feel the explosion as you throw your body forward, smell the perspiration on the other player's body. When you can do that, you're really there."

Mental rehearsal is believed to work the way physically repeating an activity does: It reinforces the messages sent from the brain to the muscles, coordinating a movement. In one study, electrodes were attached to a downhill skier who was asked to replay each moment of a race in his mind. Bursts of muscle activity were recorded by the electrodes as he envisioned hitting a jump or a rough part of the course.

The gymnast, says Olympic champion Mary Lou Retton, must practice her routines again and again until she doesn't have to think about them. "You should be able to do your entire routine sound asleep in your pajamas," she once said. "Without one mistake."

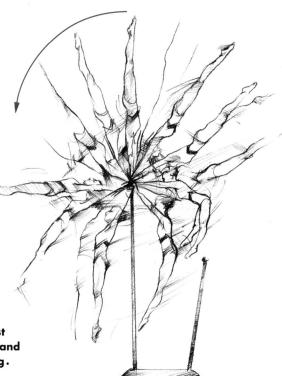

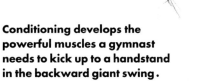

Conditioning develops the powerful muscles a gymnast needs to kick up to a handstand in the backward giant swing.

Too Much of a Good Thing

In 1988, the Boston Celtics got off to their worst start in a decade. Larry Bird, the team's leading player, was grounded by two aching heels. Ten years of pro basketball, with its relentless leaping, pivoting, and running – up to six or seven miles (11 km) per game – had caught up with him at last. He had surgery to remove a bone spur in each heel that was damaging the Achilles tendon, the power train that attaches the calf muscle to the heel bone.

While "overuse" injuries like Bird's are a predictable part of the game for professional players, doctors have been surprised to find in recent years that overuse is a major cause of sports-related injuries among young people, too.

One reason is that more and more kids are specializing at an earlier age. Instead of varying the demands on their bodies with soccer in the fall, basketball in the winter, and track in the spring, they may do the same sport year-round. And they work hard. Today, a nine-year old athlete may be asked to swim 7,000 yards (6,400 m) a day, a good training workout for a college swimmer ten years ago.

Teenagers are more vulnerable to injury than adults or younger children, says Dr. Arthur Pappas of the University of Massachusetts Medical Center. During growth spurts, their bones can grow faster than the muscles that move them, making young athletes less flexible than usual. Most important of all, the "growth plate" at the end of long bones – the part of the bone where all growth occurs – is particularly weak and vulnerable to damage just before a growth spurt.

The price of an injury to the growth plate can be steep. In some cases the injury permanently interferes with growth, causing the hurt arm or leg to remain shorter than the other one. Gymnasts who repeatedly land on their hands in the vault and floor exercises may damage the growth plates in their wrists, so that the two bones in the lower arm grow unevenly. Promising young baseball pitchers are the ones most likely to get "Little League elbow," damage to the growth plate in the upper arm bone that can restrict motion in the elbow for good. To save the arms of the future, the Little League now limits the number of pitches a player can throw each week.

Dr. Pappas recommends that coaches watch their young athletes for signs of accelerated growth, so that they can temporarily ease up on training. And young people who have "growing pains" should listen to what their bodies are saying.

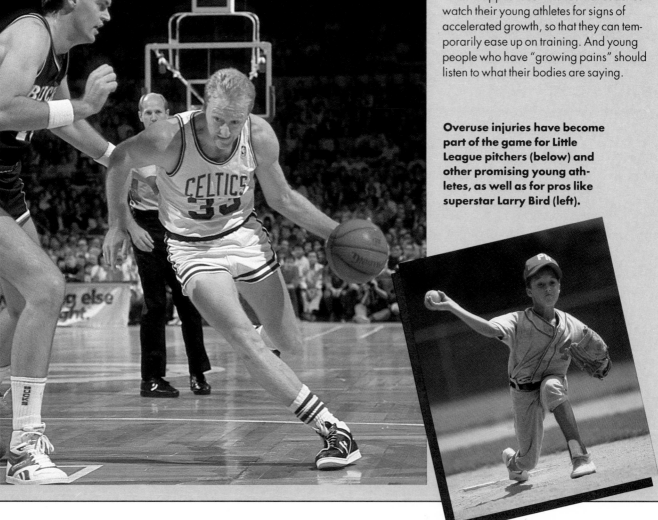

Overuse injuries have become part of the game for Little League pitchers (below) and other promising young athletes, as well as for pros like superstar Larry Bird (left).

Sports psychology offers a number of other tools for helping athletes fulfill their potential. One of them is goal-setting, used during training. The athlete focuses not on winning but on attaining specific goals, like running the 400-meter in one minute flat, and then outlines the steps needed to do that.

In competition, athletes can use various relaxation techniques to free themselves of negative emotions that can drag down a performance. Massimo teaches his gymnasts to do special breathing exercises, or picture scenes that make them feel calm. Pitcher Orel Hershiser, who led the Dodgers to an unexpected victory in the 1988 World Series, softly sang hymns before he approached the mound.

Some athletes use "biofeedback" to reduce stress reactions previously believed to be beyond conscious control. Fear and anxiety prompt the brain to release hormones that make the heart pound, the palms sweat, and muscles clench in the neck and shoulders. But with the help of electronic equipment, athletes are learning to lower their heart rate, stop sweating, and reduce unnecessary muscle tension so they can focus their energy on performance.

The stress of competition is not all bad, points out Massimo. In the right proportion, it can provide that spark of electricity that heightens an athlete's senses, quickens her reflexes, and makes her muscles move faster. This unity of mind and matter, when the body responds almost instinctively, is called "peak performance."

Ace relief pitcher Dennis Eckersley of the Oakland Athletics describes the feeling of peak performance. He says that in the rare moments when the adrenalin is flowing and everything is just right, he feels almost invincible. "There are times when I think I can spot a ball right where I want to, and the batter won't be able to hit it . . . when what I think will happen does happen. I'm so zoned on the glove, where the ball's going to go, and the catcher's mask, that either the batter won't swing, or he'll swing and miss. It doesn't matter," he says with excitement. "I just wait for the umpire's right hand to come up. You're out!"

"At least half the job is mental," says Oakland's ace reliever Dennis Eckersley, who "psyched-out" enough batters to lead the American League in 1988 with forty-nine saves.

New Hope for the Knee

Mike Stott, star quarterback and hope of the New Bedford football team, took the snap at his own thirty-two yard line and spun to the right for a pass. He wanted this win. At stake was the Southeastern Massachusetts Conference Championship, the last game of his high-school career, and the Thanksgiving Day game against arch rival Durfee High. He looked for a receiver, but they were all covered. So he tucked the ball under his arm, cut to the left to avoid a defender, and sprinted sixty-eight yards untouched to the end zone for the team's second touchdown.

Only one year before, Michael had watched the Thanksgiving game from the sidelines. He had had an outstanding sophomore season, ranking among the state's top three high school quarterbacks in passing yardage and figuring in at least one touchdown every game. But he spent the next fall nursing a knee that he hurt during preseason football camp. Thanks to new techniques in sports medicine, the injury would cost him one season instead of his athletic career.

Football is sometimes called a "collision" sport, but like many other knee injuries, Michael's occurred without any contact at all. He was rolling to the left for a pass when his cleats grabbed the grass, anchoring his foot to the ground. "My knee twisted and I felt three pops," he recalls. "They sounded like cracking your knuckles. I walked off the field, and the trainer iced down my knee. I didn't think it was too serious. But that night my knee swelled up like a balloon, and I could hardly get out of bed the next morning."

Michael went to a local sports medicine clinic the next day. The doctor gently wiggled Michael's knee to see if there was too much movement in the joint. His diagnosis: Michael had torn the anterior cruciate ligament in his knee, which keeps the shinbone from sliding out in front of the thighbone. Now believed to be one of the most serious knee injuries an athlete can sustain, it would keep Michael out the whole season. "I was devastated," confesses the five-foot eleven-inch, 185-pound (1.8-m, 84-kg) athlete. "I had a good cry."

Opposite: Michael Stott, seventeen, warms up before the Thanksgiving Day game.

One year after limping off the field with a serious knee injury, Michael made a comeback wearing a protective brace (below).

The Knee

Football players taking a hit, basketball players leaping for a rebound, downhill skiers who catch the inside of their skis – these are just a few of the athletes who account for nearly 300,000 sports-related knee injuries each year. After the oft-sprained ankle, the knee is the part of the body most frequently injured in sports.

The knee joint is like a hinge, formed by the thighbone, called the *femur,* and the shinbone, called the *tibia.* The top of the shinbone has two shallow holes scooped out of it and a ridge in between. The femur rides atop like a cowboy in a saddle. The bones would fly apart just as easily as a tossed rider were it not for a system of ligaments that straps the joint together. These ligaments include the *medial* and *lateral collateral ligaments,* which keep the knee from bending sideways; and the *cruciate ligaments,* which keep the lower leg from sliding forward or backward under the femur.

The knee acts both as a hinge and a lever, exerting enough force to power a sprinter across the finish line or a football through the goalpost. The power begins with the *quadriceps,* the largest and strongest muscle in the body, which tapers into the *quadriceps tendon* that connects to the kneecap *(patella)* and is then attached to the lower legbone by the *patella tendon.* You can imagine the kneecap as a pulley with the two tendons acting as the ropes. The quadriceps muscle helps hold the kneecap up in its place, with the entire weight of the body pressing down upon it. Simply walking down the stairs subjects your knee to three times your body weight, a full squat to more than seven times your body weight. For an adult male, that's about 1,000 pounds per square inch (70 kg/square cm).

Michael's parents took him to see Dr. Lyle Micheli, an orthopedic surgeon and 1988 president of the American College of Sports Medicine. He admitted Michael to the Children's Hospital Medical Center in Boston that night and scheduled him for arthroscopic surgery the next morning. Not many teenagers need this type of surgery. The "arthroscope," a kind of miniature telescope for looking into joints, would help the surgeon look right inside his patient's knee to see how bad the injury was.

Not long ago, Michael's injury might have been handled more casually, but with potentially disastrous results. "If Michael had come in ten years ago, he would have been told he had a sprained knee and been put in a splint for a short period of time

Right Knee (left side)

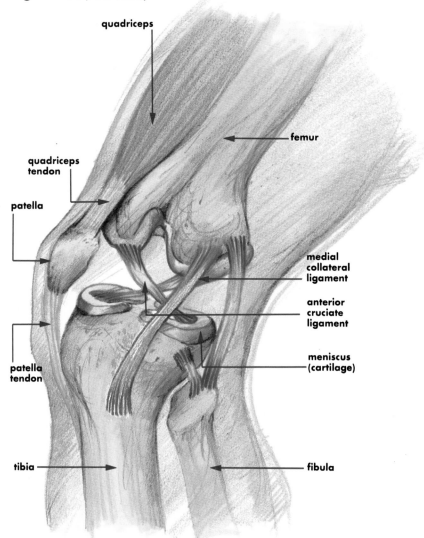

quadriceps

femur

quadriceps tendon

patella

medial collateral ligament

anterior cruciate ligament

meniscus (cartilage)

patella tendon

tibia

fibula

until he felt more comfortable," explains Dr. Micheli. "He almost certainly would have been allowed to return to play after a few weeks. That's when, I'm afraid, he would have gotten the big injury. I've heard the story so many times. The anterior cruciate ligament is initially weakened by a partial injury and then *bang* – a second injury blows out the knee."

The Arthroscope

Better treatment, says Dr. Micheli, has resulted from revolutionary techniques for peering into the hidden recesses of the human body. New computer-assisted technology, with exotic names like CAT scans and magnetic resonance imaging (MRI), helps doctors diagnose injuries with surprising accuracy. For the knee, the arthroscope has been the most useful of all. It reveals not only bones but also soft tissues, like muscles and ligaments, that are invisible in X rays. And it can be used for treatment, as well. Once the instrument has been inserted in the joint, the physician can perform an operation.

Like any other form of surgery, arthroscopy carries some risks. But it also involves less scarring and a shorter recuperation than open surgery. Dancer Mikhail Baryshnikov, Mary Lou Retton, Ivan Lendl, and Roger Clemens have all had it. In 1984 Joan Benoit Samuelson had it on her right knee and won the trial for the first women's Olympic marathon only seventeen days later.

On Wednesday morning Michael was wheeled into the operating room and "put to sleep" with a general anesthetic. Then Dr. Micheli began the operation. He made a tiny incision about one-quarter inch (6 mm) long in one of the two soft spots beneath Michael's left kneecap, and inserted the arthroscope.

This high-tech instrument has a tiny telescopic lens that is placed in the pencil-thin viewing tube at an angle. That way it offers a view around the corners formed by ligaments and bone surfaces and into the very back of the knee, where doctors could not see before. One surgeon compares the process to finding out what's behind a closed door. If you open the door a crack, you can only see part of the room. That's what open surgery is like. But if you could insert a wide-angle lens through the keyhole, you would see everything. That, he explains, is arthroscopy.

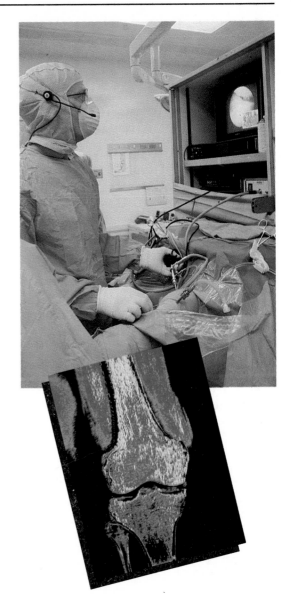

Revolutionary techniques for peering into the human body are helping doctors diagnose and treat injuries better. During arthroscopic surgery (above), the surgeon inserts a tiny telescopic lens into the knee, then views the interior of the joint on a TV screen. Below, the knee is pictured by magnetic resonance imaging (MRI), which uses radio waves and a strong magnetic field to penetrate the body without an incision.

Born Too Soon?

Does sports medicine affect the course of sports history? To answer this question, consider how many Stanley Cups the Boston Bruins might have won if Hall of Famer Bobby Orr hadn't had to leave hockey because of a bad knee.

In 1967, his second season with the Bruins, Orr injured his knee in a game against the Toronto Maple Leafs. "My left leg was pinned against the boards," he recalls. "My knee twisted and the cartilage tore." Over the next nine years, Orr would lead the Bruins to two Stanley Cup championships and win the heart of an entire city with his dazzling and unpredictable moves on the ice. But his left knee was never the same. Six operations and one arthroscopic procedure later, Bobby Orr retired at age twenty-nine.

"If arthroscopic surgery had been around years ago, would I still be playing?" asks Number 4. "The procedure is so much easier than open surgery. Each time your knee is opened up, it gets weaker. I don't think there's any question that if arthroscopy had been around, I would have played longer."

Arthroscopy might have lengthened Bobby Orr's career.

The arthroscope also contains its own light source, a fiber-optic cable made of light-transmitting threads of glass. When arthroscopy was first introduced, the surgeon looked through an eyepiece. Today, Dr. Micheli can clip onto the arthroscope a color TV camera no bigger than the palm of his hand, and watch magnified images of the interior of the knee flash onto a video screen. He can also work with long, skinny instruments specially designed to fit through an incision half the width of a fingernail – little knives, scissors, forceps, and even a motorized burr, a kind of combination sander and vacuum cleaner for smoothing torn cartilage.

Inspecting Michael's knee, Dr. Micheli was pleased to find that the tear in the ligament was partial, not all the way through. Some larger ligaments can be sewn back together again, but the fibers of the anterior cruciate hold stitches no better than a handful of spaghetti. Michael's ligament would heal best with time and a brace, Dr. Micheli concluded, not surgical repair.

Through the arthroscope, he also discovered damage to the meniscus, the thick, crescent-shaped piece of cartilage that pads the top of the shinbone. He trimmed the torn edges because they can act like sandpaper, grinding away at the joint surface and possibly leading to arthritis later in life. If pieces of cartilage break off, they can stick in the joint and make the knee jam or buckle.

Years ago, opening up the knee was such a major operation that doctors usually took out the whole meniscus to make sure no troublesome pieces remained. Today, they simply trim away the torn area. Michael's surgery took only an hour, and he went home the next morning. If his ligament could have been fixed as easily as the cartilage, he probably would have been running within three or four weeks and playing in the last football games of the season. Instead, he faced months of physical therapy to regain mobility and strength in his knee.

Bracing Himself

The moment he stepped out of the hospital with his leg in a brace and crutches under his armpits, Michael began working toward playing football in 1988. "Football means everything to me," says the seventeen-year-old. "I've been playing all my life."

When he first went out for football during his freshman year, "Michael was a very small, frail kid," recalls New Bedford High's football coach, Joseph Wirth. But a year of growing and working out three afternoons in the weight room changed that.

The next fall "Michael came back bigger and stronger. He had a lot of zip on the ball. I had a senior as quarterback, but Mike stepped right out and battled for position. He got it," says Wirth, who has coached at Brown, Holy Cross, Colgate, and Union College. "His accomplishment that year was phenomenal, to come in as a sophomore and take the team to a 7-1-2 season."

Michael approached his rehabilitation with the same zeal and determination he used to take to a game. He practiced flexing and straightening his knee, and went swimming every day. And instead of spending the afternoon with his friends at football practice, he went to physical therapy sessions three times a week.

Michael discusses the next play with quarterback coach John Seed. Michael's enthusiasm and leadership, said his coaches, instilled confidence in the team.

Under Construction

Fans wondered if basketball star Bernard King would play again after he injured his knee in 1985. Four years after having his knee rebuilt in an operation called "anterior cruciate ligament reconstruction," he is one of the Washington Bullets' top scorers. Running back Curt Warner had the operation, and went on to become the Seattle Seahawks' all-time leading rusher in yards, attempts, and touchdowns.

The knee can be rebuilt with tissue borrowed from other parts of the leg: the hamstring tendon, kneecap tendon, or tissue from the thigh, for example. Not everyone with torn ligaments needs the operation. With or without it, the athlete has to work hard to regain the use of his knee. Warner spent a whole year doing rehabilitation exercises before playing football again. He even learned how to swim!

In another technique, the anterior cruciate ligament is replaced with braids of Gore-Tex or Dacron. These high-strength materials have been approved by the federal government for use in people who have already had one knee reconstruction that failed. Doctors suspect that sooner or later the artificial ligaments will break from all the wear and tear in the knee, but no one knows yet how many years that will take.

There he rode the stationary bike, lifted weights to stay in shape, and kept on exercising his knee. After the range of motion in the joint improved, he began to strengthen the surrounding muscles. He trained the hamstring muscles in the back of his thigh to take over for the weakened ligament and hold the shinbone in place. He exercised with leg weights and worked out on a Biodex machine, similar to the Cybex Siri used to rehabilitate her elbow.

The hardest thing of all was "accepting that I couldn't play the '87 season," said Michael, who cheered on his teammates at every game wearing the same good-luck clothes. "It hurt to go to the games, seeing the team and feeling that I could have helped out," he says.

Just when he was feeling worst, he received a letter from New England Patriots' quarterback Steve Grogan, who has sustained more than his share of injuries during his fourteen-year career. "You can come back from this. Be positive, work hard, and listen to your doctor," wrote Grogan. He had heard about Michael from Joe Wirth, who briefly coached the Patriots. "Believe me, if you stay positive, give it 110 percent, and believe you can come back – you will."

◀
Bernard King made a successful court comeback with a rebuilt knee.

A lightweight plastic brace keeps Michael's knee from shifting, but gives him the freedom to run and pivot.

In mid-November Michael cast aside his crutches and switched to a smaller, lighter leg brace. It still kept his knee from twisting, but it could be adjusted to allow him to straighten his leg all the way. He could even jog while wearing it. Only fifteen years ago braces for legs, backs, and other parts of the body were made of rubber and metal and were far too cumbersome to wear playing sports. Now lightweight plastic braces hold a joint firmly in place while allowing the athlete to move as much as possible.

Because of his dedication, Michael recovered more quickly than expected. By the end of December, his left leg was as strong as his right. He was ready to compete again, this time at a new sport: track. In the spring, he placed fifth in the 100-meter at the state championships. But he was dreaming of football. To get ready, he devoted his summer afternoons to running, swimming, bike riding, and pumping iron.

He had his doctor's go-ahead to attend preseason football camp in July as long as he wore a knee brace whenever he played. Not just for that summer, but for good. The brace would protect his knee against direct hits and prevent twisting movements that might harm the weakened ligament.

"If young people adequately rehabilitate and protect the knee, it will heal and function quite well," said Dr. Micheli. "But it will never be 100 percent." Once stretched, the ligament stays stretched; it will never hold the joint as tightly as it did before.

Michael returned to the playing field wearing a shoe called the Tanel 360, which has a large ring instead of cleats beneath the ball of the foot. It helps prevent knee injuries by allowing the foot to pivot instead of getting stuck in the ground. The shoe was designed by Mike Tanel, a college defensive end whose plans for a pro career ended after he wrenched his knee wrestling a running back to the ground.

Wearing his cleatless shoes and the knee brace, Michael steered the Whalers to a 27-0 victory Thanksgiving Day with his parents, brothers, aunts, uncles, and cousins cheering in the stands. As he starts to think about colleges, his big question is where, not whether, he will play next season.

Michael celebrates his final high school football victory. Thanks to new techniques in sports medicine, his injury cost him one season rather than his entire career.

▶
Michael's shoe, the Tanel 360, has a ring instead of cleats beneath the ball of the foot. It was designed to prevent injuries by allowing the foot to pivot more easily.

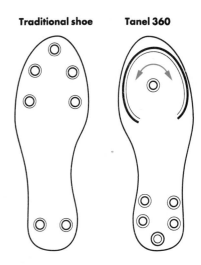

Traditional shoe   Tanel 360

Who Gets Hurt

**Injuries by position
(per 100 games) in 1988**

Position		Value
Running Back	🏈🏈🏈🏈🏈🏈🏈🏈	8.3
Quarterback	🏈🏈🏈🏈🏈🏈	6.6
Defensive Lineman	🏈🏈🏈🏈	4.6
Wide Receiver	🏈🏈🏈🏈	4.4
Linebacker	🏈🏈🏈🏈	4.3
Offensive Lineman	🏈🏈🏈	3.1
Tight End	🏈🏈🏈	2.7
Defensive Back	🏈🏈🏈	2.7

When Players Get Hurt

60% Practice

40% Game

Source: National Athletic Trainers' Association

▲

As players get bigger, faster, and stronger, the game of football is getting rougher at all levels, from high school to the NFL. The National Athletic Trainers' Association estimates that in 1988, about one-third of high school football players were injured. Sixty pecent of the injuries, like Michael's, occurred during practice rather than a game.

Playing It Safe

Of the one million United States high school students who played football in 1988, more than a third were injured badly enough to stop playing for at least a day, according to a study by the National Athletic Trainers' Association (NATA). Because some students were injured more than once, the organization estimated that more than a half million injuries occurred.

While most of the injuries were minor – sprains, strains, bruises, and the like – NATA estimates that about 65,000 injuries took three weeks or longer to heal, and about 13,000 required surgery. Nearly two-thirds of these operations were on the knee.

To make football and other high school sports safer, NATA urges schools to hire an athletic trainer to provide emergency treatment and supervise injury prevention and rehabilitation. The trainer should be present not only at games but also at practices, where 60 percent of high school football injuries occur.

Here are a few steps you can take to avoid injury:

• Wear protective equipment that is in good condition and fits properly. The number of high school players paralyzed from football injuries fell from thirty-four in 1975 to five in 1984 thanks to improvements in the design of football helmets and new rules that banned "spearing," or using the head as a battering ram.

• Don't play when you're hurt or if you haven't fully recovered. As many as 20 percent of sports injuries may be re-injuries.

• Play on teams organized by size and ability level, not just age. Boys can have their major growth spurt at any time from the eighth to tenth grade, and may vary from each other in height by a foot (0.3 m) or more.

• Warm up and stretch before playing. Dr. Micheli also recommends a well-supervised program of weight training three times a week year-round to develop the muscular strength needed to protect joints from injury.

• Drink fluids during play, particularly in warm weather, to keep from getting overheated. Fluids should never be denied to players as a form of discipline.

• Find a well-trained coach who stresses values and learning the game, not just winning.

• Have a preseason physical examination to catch health problems. Undetected heart problems are believed to cause several sports-related deaths in young people each year. The exam also can assess how close your bones are to full growth. Some physicians recommend that teenagers stay away from collision sports, like ice hockey and tackle football, until the long bones of the arms and legs have stopped growing.

Sports medicine, points out Dr. Micheli, is not just repairing injuries. It's trying to prevent them in the first place.

RICE

Next time you suffer from a sprained ankle or a pulled muscle, just remember one word: RICE. The letters stand for Rest, Ice, Compression, and Elevation; and they spell the best first-aid recipe for sprains, bruises, and many other common sports injuries.

Resting the hurt ankle, knee, or whatever you have injured keeps it from getting worse. Ice, compression, and elevation all fight swelling, which causes pain and slows down recovery by limiting movement. The ice shrinks blood vessels so that bleeding inside the joint is reduced. Elevating the hurt limb above the level of the heart ensures that blood and other fluids can drain away rather than pool around the injury. And compression – wrapping or taping the injury – helps maintain the normal shape of the joint or limb. Although you might think that a hot bath would make a sore ankle or elbow feel better, heat increases blood flow and makes the swelling worse.

Some doctors call their treatment plan "PRICE," adding a "P" for the protection offered by splints, casts, or crutches. Injuries like fractures, strained muscles, and torn ligaments may need to be kept immobile to aid healing and prevent further damage.

◄
For Patriots quarterback Steve Grogan, the benefits of playing football far outweigh the risks. "Football teaches a lot of great values: discipline, teamwork, confidence, so many things you can apply to life that you don't learn unless you're part of a team working toward a common goal," he says. "If you train and condition and study the game, you lessen the risk of being hurt."

The Limits of Endurance

At four A.M. on April 23, 1988, cyclist Glenn Tremml awoke in a dark hotel room on a small volcanic island called Santorini off the coast of Greece. As the sun rose, he climbed to a mountaintop radio station and peered across the Aegean Sea toward Crete. There, seventy-four miles (119 km) away, his colleague Kanellos Kanellopoulos, a member of Greece's Olympic cycling team, was preparing for a test of space-age engineering and age-old brawn. In a few hours he would try to pedal to Santorini in a super-light aircraft called *Daedalus 88*, using only his own muscles to power the flight.

With a wingspan greater than that of a Boeing 727, the aircraft weighed only sixty-eight pounds (31 kg), less than half as much as its pilot. Its skeleton was made of an experimental graphite material as strong as aluminum but even lighter; the body, or fuselage, of Kevlar, the plastic used in bulletproof vests. To cut down on the air drag that would be caused by an open cockpit, the pilot would be sealed into the craft with a sheet of Mylar about as thick as the plastic wrap you use on sandwiches. He would lean back in a beach loungelike chair, his legs extended to reach the pedals and a control stick at each side.

The flight was expected to take anywhere from four to six hours, depending on the unpredictable winds. As an athletic feat, it would be comparable to running two three-hour marathons back to back. But the pilot could never rest. If he stopped pedaling for even a moment, the plane's propeller would stop turning, and he would splash down into the sea.

Five top cyclists, including Tremml and Kanellopoulos, had been training nine months for this moment. Many more were rejected because they were not fit enough. As Tremml scanned the horizon this morning, he could see that after three weeks of high winds, the weather finally was right. "The ocean was as flat as a sheet of glass. When the sun rose and I saw how calm it was, I knew Kanellos could make it," he said.

Opposite: Greek national cycling champion Kanellos Kanellopolous trains for the Daedalus flight.

Daedulus '88 had a wingspan greater than that of a Boeing 727 jet, but weighed only sixty-eight pounds (31 kg), less than half as much as its pilot.

Daedalus pilots, left to right: Kanellos Kanellopolous, Erik Schmidt, Frank Scioscia, Glenn Tremml, Greg Zack.

The route had been chosen to recreate the mythical flight of Daedalus (Dé-da-lus), a Greek inventor and craftsman imprisoned on the island of Crete some 3,500 years ago. According to one version of the legend, he fashioned wings of wax and feathers so that he and his son, Icarus, could escape. While Daedalus flew safely home, Icarus was carried away with his newfound power and flew too close to the sun. His wings melted and he crashed into the sea. Would Kanellos get a dunking, as well? Or could he generate the power needed to complete the flight?

The Human Engine

When engineers at the Massachusetts Institute of Technology undertook the Daedalus Project in 1985, the world record for human-powered flight was held by Bryan Allen in the *Gossamer Albatross*. He had barely been able to finish the three-hour, twenty-two-mile (35-km) flight across the English Channel. Assistant

Why Birds Can Fly – and People Can't

Like Daedalus in the myth, humans throughout history have strapped handmade wings to their arms, but could never get their weighty frames far off the ground. The body of the bird, on the other hand, is exquisitely designed for flight. Its strong but lightweight wings provide a large surface area for air to flow over, creating a difference in air pressure above and below the wing that helps lift the bird off the ground.

To keep down the weight the wings must carry aloft, the bird's torpedo-shaped body is stripped to the essentials. Even its bones are filled with hollow spaces. It has a fast metabolism and a souped-up heart rate that can speed oxygen to working muscles. In small birds like the robin, the heart beats as fast as 600 times a minute. Propulsion comes from the bird's powerful chest and wing muscles, which can make up as much as a quarter of the bird's body weight. In contrast, the chest muscles of a man make up less than 1 percent of his weight. His most powerful muscles, the quadriceps, are in his legs. That's why the Daedalus pilots had to pedal rather than flap when they took to the air.

aeronautics professor Steven Bussolari, the Daedalus Project's director of flight operations, knew the MIT team could design a more efficient aircraft. But was it physically possible for a pilot to pedal three times as far? Scientists have studied marathon running, and their findings have helped improve training. But there was little data on exercise lasting as long as four to six hours, the estimated time of the flight. So Bussolari consulted Ethan Nadel, professor of physiology at the Yale University School of Medicine, for an answer.

To perform their calculations, they regarded the pilot as the craft's engine, his body as a machine. Like the engine in a car or plane, he would need fuel, or food, to keep going; oxygen to burn the fuel; and water to stay cool. Given the design of the plane, they determined the pilot must produce about one-third horsepower throughout the flight just to keep the propeller turning. Very few adults can do that much work for so long. It's not just because their muscles are not strong enough. Their heart and lungs are not strong enough, either.

Fast Twitch, Slow Twitch

Muscle fibers come in two types. *Slow-twitch fibers*, which are red, contract less forcefully than *fast-twitch fibers* but can keep working for longer periods of time. They are filled with mitochondria, the power plants in the cell where oxygen is used to produce energy. The white fast-twitch fibers are more powerful but fatigue easily.

Olympic marathon runner Bill Rodgers reportedly has about 80 percent slow-twitch fibers in his legs. On the other hand, athletes with a high percentage of fast-twitch fibers have a natural advantage in sports like gymnastics or weight lifting, which require power. The distribution of fast and slow fibers in a muscle is determined at birth. But new research indicates that with training, some fast-twitch fibers develop the capacity to work longer by using oxygen to burn fuel.

The flight route (below) was based on the mythical flight of Daedalus and his son Icarus, who in ancient times tried to escape Crete on wings of wax and feathers (left).

SANTORINI

Planned flight route (74 miles/119 km)

Knossos

CRETE

The Heart of an Athlete

Exercise transforms the body, and the type of exercise determines the shape you take. The Daedalus flight was a test of endurance, and pilots were selected on the strength of their hearts and lungs.

With endurance training, like running or cycling long distances, your body gradually changes so that it can supply more oxygen to your muscles. The chest muscles grow stronger, so more air is pumped in and out of the lungs with each breath. The heart muscle grows larger and stronger, arteries widen, and more blood can flow through. The body manufactures extra blood and more oxygen-carrying red cells. This increase in blood volume actually stretches the heart so that it springs back harder with each beat, like a taut rubber band. As a result, the "stroke volume," or amount of blood sent from the heart to the rest of the body with each beat, increases dramatically.

In short, the heart can beat more slowly and still deliver more oxygen to the cells. Not only can the trained athlete exercise harder and longer without getting winded,

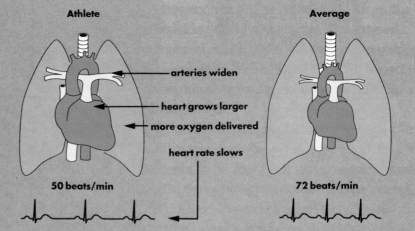

Athlete

arteries widen
heart grows larger
more oxygen delivered
heart rate slows

50 beats/min

Average

72 beats/min

but he also has improved his health. An endurance athlete may have a resting "heart rate" (the number of times the heart beats per minute) about twenty beats below average. That saves the heart work – more than ten million beats per year.

Exercise also improves the body's ability to remove oxygen from the blood. New blood vessels, called "capillaries," grow in the muscle tissue, and the chemistry of the cells changes. The peak rate at which the body can take in and use oxygen is called "VO$_2$ max."

The athlete built for endurance sports has fewer fast-twitch muscles in his legs than average. Endurance training itself seems to detract from leg speed and power; one marathon runner with a vertical jump of only twelve inches (30 cm) could jump twenty inches (51 cm) after he stopped competing. Weight lifters train their muscles for explosive power, but their hearts generally cannot pump as much blood as the hearts of marathon runners. They don't need to. A single lift requires enormous muscular strength, but lasts for less than a second.

	Average U.S. Male	Daedalus Pilots	Weight lifter
height	5'10" (1.77 m)	5'10" (1.77 m)	5'8" (1.73 m)
VO$_2$ max	35-40 ml O$_2$/kg/min	70 ml O$_2$/kg/min	45 ml O$_2$/kg/min
stroke volume	100 ml	175 ml	145 ml
resting heart rate	72 beats/min	50 beats/min	65 beats/min
weight	160 lbs (72.5 kg)	145 lbs (66 kg)	190 lbs (86 kg)
body fat	20 percent	5-10 percent	15 percent
slow twitch fibers in legs	50 percent	70-80 percent (estimated)	45 percent

100 milliliters (ml) = 3.38 fluid ounces
1 liter (L) = 1.05 quarts
1 kilogram (kg) = 2.2 pounds

Figures are averages based on various studies

Some people are naturally suited to "endurance" events, like marathon running or a long-distance bicycle race, because they were born with more "slow-twitch" than "fast-twitch" muscle fibers in their legs. Muscles make us move by contracting, and slow-twitch fibers contract only half as quickly as fast ones. But although they are slower, they have the chemical machinery needed to contract over and over again without getting tired.

Each time muscles contract, they produce mechanical work (pedaling, in the case of the Daedalus pilots) and heat. The energy needed to do this work comes from the food we eat. The most important sources of energy for exercise are carbohydrates, which include sugars, like fruit, and starches, like bread and rice. Inside the body, all carbohydrates are broken down into a type of sugar molecule called "glucose" before they can be used as fuel. Muscles can burn glucose directly or store it in the form of long chains called "glycogen."

When muscles use oxygen to convert glucose into energy, the process is called "aerobic" energy production. The condition of our heart and lungs – in other words, how fit we are – determines how much oxygen we can deliver to our muscles and how long we can keep exercising.

When we need extra power for an intense spurt of exercise– to lift a weight or burst across the finish line – the aerobic system can't keep up. The muscles begin to burn glucose without oxygen. This is called the "anaerobic" energy pathway. Most people can maintain anaerobic exercise for only a few minutes at a time, because it leaves behind a waste product called lactic acid that makes muscles ache and get tired.

If too much lactic acid builds up, the muscles stop working and we slow down. The body tries to take in more oxygen so it can remove the lactic acid by burning it for fuel. When we huff and puff, we are trying to take in more air and repay an "oxygen debt" that built up during exertion.

▶

Top: Muscles can convert food into energy with or without oxygen. But exercise without oxygen can't be maintained long because its waste product, lactic acid, makes muscles tired.

Bottom: This chart shows that the longer we exercise the

more we rely on oxygen for energy. The aerobic pathway can't provide the burst of power needed for a 100-meter sprint, but it can keep a runner's legs pumping for a 26.2-mile (42.2-km) marathon. For most events, the two energy pathways work together.

Energy Pathways...

anaerobic
(no oxygen)

aerobic
(oxygen)

Lactic acid builds up in blood. Muscles stop working.

Carbon dioxide and water are exhaled. Exercise can continue.

...And When We Use Them

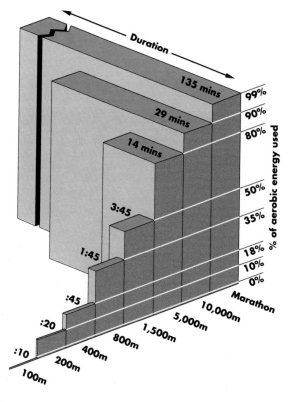

The portrait of the pilot was becoming clear. Traditionally, attempts at human-powered flight have used very experienced pilots. For Daedalus, only a world-class athlete would do. Nadel and Bussolari needed to find a pilot who could deliver enough oxygen to his muscles to keep them pumping on aerobic energy alone.

Because the aircraft would be pedaled they narrowed their pilot search to cyclists, athletes who had already trained the specific muscle groups required. Three hundred cyclists, several of Olympic caliber, applied for the job. Twenty-four men and one woman were invited to Nadel's lab to take a test on a "cycle ergometer," an exercise bike that measures energy output. While the athletes pedaled as hard as they could, the scientists measured how much oxygen they consumed.

Eleven athletes were selected for further screening. The amount of oxygen they could deliver to their muscles was nearly twice that of the average male. It looked like they could make the flight with energy to spare.

The Daedalus Drink

Only about one-fourth of the energy humans produce during exercise actually moves muscles and bones. The rest is wasted as heat. Nadel estimated that the Daedalus pilot would generate enough heat during the flight to raise his body temperature one degree Centigrade every five minutes. "If your body didn't have any mechanism for getting rid of heat," says the physiologist, "you could only exercise at that rate for fifteen minutes before you would get so overheated your brain would stop working."

A series of tests in Ethan Nadel's lab helped select the most efficient human engines for the flight (left). The tests also showed that the pilot would need an energy-boosting drink to keep from running out of fuel, and more air-flow in the tiny cockpit (right) to keep from over-heating.

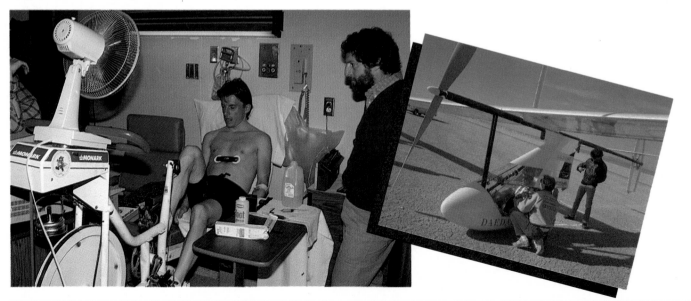

Luckily, the body does have mechanisms for getting rid of heat. As blood circulates through the body, it carries heat away from the body core and up to the skin, where it is transferred to the environment in the form of sweat. But if the water is not replaced, the body starts to overheat.

Nadel estimated that during the flight the pilot would sweat away about one quart (0.95 L) of water each hour. He would lose well over ten pounds (4.5 kg) during the flight unless the same amount of fluid was replaced. During most types of exercise, drinking water is a good way to replace fluid. But the Daedalus pilot would lose so much salt in his sweat that he would need to replace salt, as well.

Finally, the pilot would need extra fuel to "top off" his supplies of glycogen, a form of sugar stored right on the muscle fibers. Glycogen is the main source of energy used during exercise. With training and good nutrition, an athlete can more than double the amount of glycogen stored by the muscles. Even so, he may run out of fuel two or so hours into a race, an experience called "hitting the wall" by runners and "bonking" by cyclists.

How Muscles Contract

The muscles we use for movement are bundles of individual *fibers*, single cells that stretch all the way from one end of the muscle to the other. These fibers are made from thinner strands called *myofibrils*, which in turn are made up of tiny threads of protein called *actin* and *myosin*.

These threads are covered with little knobs and notches. When the muscle receives a signal from the brain to contract, the threads slide past each other and the knobs and notches interlock like fingers. The ends of the muscle are pulled closer together. Well-trained muscles can contract by half their length.

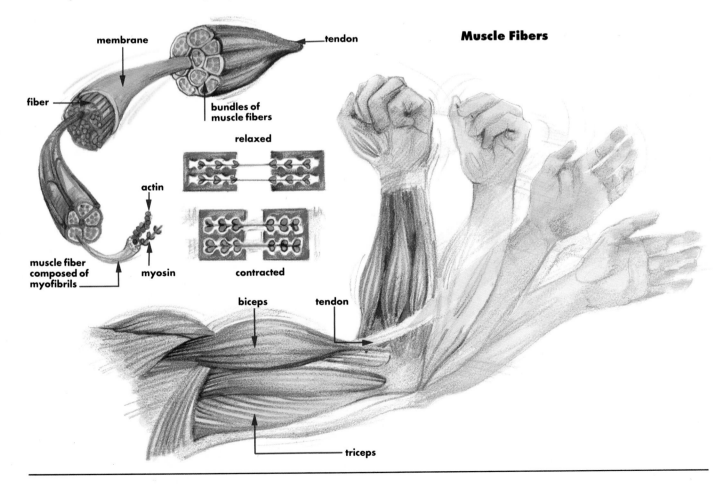

membrane

tendon

fiber

bundles of muscle fibers

Muscle Fibers

actin

relaxed

muscle fiber composed of myofibrils

myosin

contracted

biceps

tendon

triceps

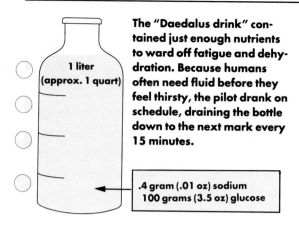

The "Daedalus drink" contained just enough nutrients to ward off fatigue and dehydration. Because humans often need fluid before they feel thirsty, the pilot drank on schedule, draining the bottle down to the next mark every 15 minutes.

1 liter (approx. 1 quart)

.4 gram (.01 oz) sodium
100 grams (3.5 oz) glucose

Exactly how much sugar, fluid, and salt would need to be replaced? Nadel asked the top eleven candidates to return for a four-hour trial of endurance. They drank one liter (a liter is approximately one quart) per hour of a commercial sport drink while the scientists monitored the chemistry of their blood.

During the last hour of the test, the pilots' blood sugar fell and their heart rate went up. Three got tired and dropped out. Nadel concluded they needed a little more sugar. Using the test results, he created a drink that contained about .4 gram sodium and 100 grams of the simple sugar glucose per liter (approximately .01 ounce sodium and 3.5 ounces glucose per quart), and tasted somewhat like weak lemonade. For the flight the brew was stored in one-liter plastic bottles with marks along the side. Every fifteen minutes, the pilot would drink down to the next mark, draining a bottle an hour.

Learning to Fly

Five pilots were selected as a result of the endurance test. All five were needed because the scientists could not predict ahead of time the exact day of the flight. The pilots would rotate their training schedules like baseball pitchers, so that there was always one pilot in peak condition for the flight.

In September Bussolari began teaching the pilots how to fly. They practiced with flight simulators, light airplanes, and gliders until they were accomplished enough to attempt a solo flight in a human-powered craft.

Pilots' meals contained less fat and red meat than the average American meal, but about three times as many calories. For long-lasting energy, the pilots loaded up on carbohydrates.

Daedalus Pilot's Dinner

Average Dinner

"It feels like you're floating on a cushion of air. It's not jerky like a ride in a jet plane – it's more like your dreams of flight," said Tremml. "You don't feel like you're moving, but you can see trucks or boats down below racing alongside. You can hear your own breathing – that's the loudest sound in the plane. It's very, very quiet."

For training, the pilots logged about 400 miles (650 km) a week on their bikes, varying their daily schedules to meet different goals. To boost their endurance, they went on long workouts of 100 miles (160 km) or more. To increase strength in their legs, they practiced climbing hills on their bikes. And to train their nervous systems to move their legs without energy-wasting movements, they practiced pedaling fast – pushing their legs at about ninety-five revolutions per minute.

Eating for Endurance

"The pilots ate a tremendous amount of food," says Bussolari. "It looked like three or four times what we would normally eat per day. It also would take three or four times as long to prepare, and three or four times as long to eat."

At the height of their training, the pilots were burning about 7,000 calories a day. (A calorie is a unit of measurement expressing the heat- or energy-producing value in food.) In comparison, American men, on the average, burn only 2,300 calories. Like teenagers, who need a nutrient-rich diet for growing bones and tissues, the pilots needed a high-quality diet to help their bodies recover from the stress of training. Their ability to withstand the rigors of the flight would depend on the quality of the food they ate in preparation.

Scientists have learned that the amount of glycogen stored in the body determines how long muscles can keep moving. Only carbohydrates, which include starches and sugars, can be used by the body to make glycogen. Therefore, an athlete can increase his or her glycogen stores by eating more carbohydrates. Les Wong, a nutritionist with the Shaklee Corporation, one of the Daedalus Project's sponsors, recommended that the Daedalus pilots eat a diet made up of about 60-70 percent carbohydrates, 10-20 percent protein, and 10-20 percent fat. In comparison, the average American's meals are 40 percent carbohydrate, 18 percent protein, and 42 percent fat.

The pilots trained by cycling 400 miles (650 km) a week. They climbed hills to develop strength, and took long rides through the countryside to build up endurance.

For take-off, the pilot pedals down the runway as crew members run alongside, holding up the long wings (top). Flying Daedalus '88, says one pilot, "feels like floating on a cushion of air."

The pilots ate lots of fruit – up to twenty-nine servings per day – which is rich in vitamins and minerals as well as quick-energy sugar. For starch they might eat three different cereals for breakfast, six slices of homemade bread for lunch, and a plate loaded with pasta for dinner. The real challenge was cutting down on fat. The pilots gave up butter and mayonnaise, cut down on red meat in favor of chicken and fish, and switched to nonfat milk. To make sure they got enough calcium, which builds strong bones, they drank as many as six glasses of milk a day.

Our bodies need a certain amount of fat to function, but for endurance athletes, carrying extra flesh is like running around with a backpack. Normally, body fat makes up 15 percent to 25 percent of body weight in adult men, and 20 percent to 30 percent of body weight in adult women. In spite of all they ate, the Daedalus pilots probably had 5 percent to 10 percent body fat, close to the minimum required for good health. (For women, a minimum of 10 percent body fat is generally recommended.)

To improve their endurance, the pilots used a technique called "carbohydrate loading." In this six-day program, the athlete uses up muscle glycogen stores with three days of intense training. For the final three days the athlete eats a high-carbohydrate diet and tapers off training. The muscles overcompensate, soaking up glycogen like a sponge. Carbohydrate loading does not help performance in sports events lasting less than an hour.

The Daedalus pilots each began the carbohydrate loading program at a different time. That way, when the wind died down and calm seas beckoned, at least one athlete would be rested and ready for the flight.

The Flight

The perfect day dawned on April 23. It was Kanellos Kanellopoulos' turn to attempt the flight. According to his colleagues, the 156-pound (70-kg), thirty-one-year-old Kanellos was a merciless competitor and a talented, dedicated athlete. "He was very serious about training," says Tremml. "He knew when to sleep, when to eat, when to rest, and when to work. He was a master."

At 7:06 A.M., Kanellos climbed into the cockpit and began pedaling down the runway. The flight went without a hitch. "As word got out on Santorini that Kanellos was coming, cars and buses of people crossed the fields and vineyards and poured onto the beach," says Tremml. "First, we could see the flashing of the propeller, then gradually the fuselage and the wing."

Just as he reached the beach, the craft was broken apart by high winds. As the plane crashed into the shallow water, Kanellos burst out of the cockpit with a smile on his face. The Daedalus team celebrated with champagne as Kanellos signed autographs on pieces of the plane.

Kanellos's flight time was a human-powered flight record of three hours and fifty-four minutes. By all accounts, he could have gone on much longer before becoming fatigued. While Tremml speculates that there could be pilots tougher and stronger than he and his colleagues, he suspects the greatest improvements in the field of human-powered flight will come from changes in aircraft design. How far can an aircraft fly with a human as its engine? The Daedalus Project is over, but other scientists and athletes doubtless will take up the challenge.

Not quite four hours after take-off, Daedalus '88 approaches Santorini (right). A wet but smiling Kanellos is escorted to shore (left). Chest electrodes monitored his heart rate for signs of fatigue during the flight.

The Computerized Athlete

Gail Conway, a twenty-six-year-old captain in the U.S. Air Force, runs on a treadmill flanked by lights, cameras, and researchers at computers. She starts at the brisk pace of a six-minute mile (1 mile=1.609 kilometers). Her feet land with a beat as even as a metronome's, and her arms pump low and steady. Every two minutes the scientists crank the treadmill speed up a notch, pushing Gail close to racing pace.

As she begins to sweat, the unforgiving eyes of two cameras are trained upon her, ready to catch any imperfection in her technique, any sign that she is suffering from fatigue. From the length of her stride, to how far she leans forward, to the angle at which her heel strikes the ground, the details of her running "mechanics" will be analyzed by computer and compared with those of some of the nation's best runners.

The treadmill analysis is only one of many tests Gail will take at a camp for "elite," or top-level, middle- and long-distance runners held at the U.S. Olympic Committee (U.S.O.C.) Training Center in the shadow of Pike's Peak in Colorado Springs. Eleven athletes from around the country are joining her at the camp in September, 1988. She saw a number of them at the Olympic trials only two months before. Now, while the victors are about to compete halfway around the world at the Summer Games in Seoul, Gail and her colleagues gather to learn how sports science might help them prevent injury and improve their performance – perhaps just enough to earn them a slot on the U.S. Olympic team in 1992.

Jay T. Kearney, director of Sports Science at the U.S.O.C., won't claim that the U.S.O.C. program has won any gold medals. The athletes do that. Kearney's staff tries to help with the fine-tuning. "If we take 1 percent of performance and help them improve that much – that's a major gain," he explains. "For an 800-meter runner like Gail whose time is 2 minutes, that would save 1.2 seconds. If she could run that, she would be in Seoul."

Opposite: Captain Gail Conway U.S.A.F., will have her running style analyzed at the U.S.O.C. Training Center.

Like the runner below, she will take the treadmill test. High-speed cameras record the runner's performance as he runs on the treadmill. Later, computer analysis of the film and videotape will detect any flaws in his technique.

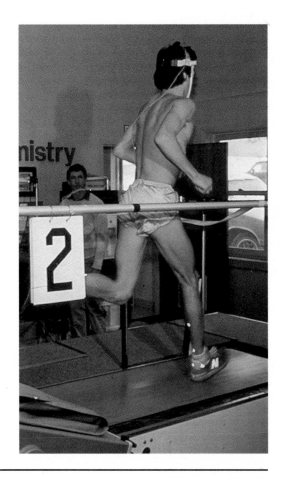

Rx for Shoulder Pain

A few months before the 1984 Winter Olympics, the pain in figure skater Peter Carruthers' shoulder became unbearable. The tip of his shoulder blade was inflamed, causing muscle spasms in his back whenever he tried to toss and catch his sister Kitty. He considered surgery, but doubted he could recover in time to compete.

Instead of submitting to the scalpel, Peter put himself at the mercy of a high-speed video camera. Dr. Arthur Pappas of the University of Massachusetts Medical Center taped him skating with Kitty. The tape was replayed in slow motion, stripping away the mystery from moves too fast for even a coach's trained eye.

"My lifting technique was not correct," Carruthers discovered with surprise. "I was letting my right shoulder come forward on the lifts, putting stress on the shoulderblade." Dr. Pappas prescribed daily exercises to strengthen the back and shoulder muscles needed to hold the joint firmly in place.

Peter Carruthers also worked with his sister and coach to re-learn the way he did lifts. "A lot of conscious thought went into each lift I did, making sure I didn't let my shoulder wing out. To this day I still have to think about it," he said. The pain gradually subsided. In February the duo won a silver medal with an electrifying performance at the Winter Olympics.

High-speed photography helped Peter and Kitty Carruthers correct their lifting technique.

One focus of the U.S.O.C.'s research is "biomechanics," a combination of anatomy, physics, and engineering. As in the Daedalus Project, scientists regard the human body as a machine – but this time as a collection of joints and levers, propelled by muscles and constrained by gravity and the laws of nature. Using the latest technology, from high-speed photography to computer processing, scientists can break down an activity into individual steps and analyze the role of each body part.

"All human movement conforms to the laws of physics," explains Sarah Smith of the U.S.O.C.'s Biomechanics Department. "Biomechanics takes Newton's formulas describing the laws of motion and applies them to describe human motion and improve human performance. Whether you are a basketball player, a gymnast, or a skater, once you are in the air you are a "projectile" – an object propelled by a force – and all the physical laws that apply to projectiles apply to you."

At the elite testing camps offered by the U.S.O.C.'s Sports Science Program, the researchers hope to transfer information from the lab to the athlete and her coach.

Balancing Act

Growing up, Gail Conway never thought of herself as an athlete. On the high school track team in Tacoma, Washington, she held her own in the 200-meter, the 440-meter relay, and the high jump. But she wasn't a star. Then, at a meet during her senior year, Gail was asked to run the 400-meter in place of an ailing teammate. She raised more than a few eyebrows when she ran the race in fifty-nine seconds flat on her first try. Three weeks later she ran two seconds faster, placing second in the state championships.

Gail began competing at the national level the next fall while attending the U.S. Air Force Academy in Colorado Springs. Now a cross-country and track coach at the Academy, she runs the 800-meter. After an exciting 1987 racing season in which she ran a personal best of 2:00.4 (2 minutes and 4/10 seconds), she began training for the Olympics. Her rigorous schedule of two intense ses-

▶
To design a training program for Gail, researchers monitor how much oxygen she consumes when she runs at different speeds (right). Blood tests taken while Gail runs show how much lactic acid builds up in her blood (left).

sions a day may have been too much, too soon for her body's capabilities. In March she developed a "stress fracture," or small crack, in her right shinbone. She donned a life vest and for two months did her running in a pool to protect her leg from impact. Still, she felt her training suffered. She qualified for the 1988 Olympic trials in Indianapolis in July but was cut during the semifinals.

To do her best in future competitions, Gail needs to find the right balance. She needs to train hard enough to reach maximum performance without training so hard that she gets injured. So, on September 10, she reports to the U.S.O.C's elite runners camp.

Over the next four days, Gail's blood and daily diet will be analyzed for any nutritional deficiencies. Her leg muscles will be tested to make sure the strength is roughly equal in the quadriceps and hamstrings, the pair of muscle groups in the thigh, lest an imbalance lead to injury. Her oxygen intake will be measured as she runs at different speeds. If she consumes more oxygen than other runners to maintain the same speed, she may be wasting precious energy with unnecessary or inefficient movements – in other words, with faulty biomechanics.

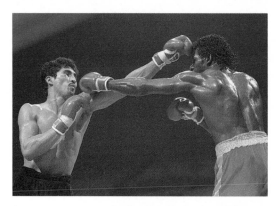

At the U.S.O.C., researchers combine studies in physiology and biomechanics to develop general training guidelines. They have found, for example, that weight training can help boxers improve the speed of their punch.

This diagram, made from measurements taken on the force platform, shows where forces are concentrated as Gail's feet hit the ground, and can help her choose the right running shoes.

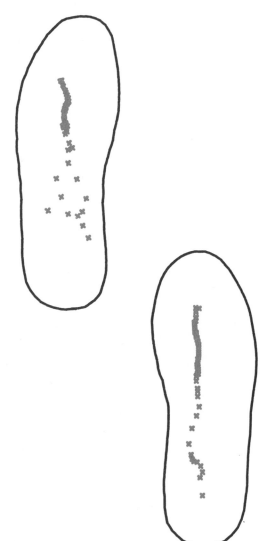

The Tests

If there are any energy-wasting flaws in Gail's technique, says Leonard Jansen, head of the U.S.O.C. Sports Science Computer Services Department, they should be identified through the following biomechanical tests:

The Force Platform. The force platform records the amount and pattern of pressure with which Gail's feet hit the ground. It is a stationary metal plate with electrical wiring underneath and small sensors, called "strain gauges," in each corner. Gail runs across the platform several times, striking it once with each pass. As her foot hits the plate, the strain gauges register changes in the voltage of the current running through them.

These electrical signals are then decoded by computer to reveal which part of Gail's foot is bearing most of the impact, and whether the force is balanced between her left and right feet. This information can help Gail select a running shoe suited to the way she runs.

Gail learns that when she runs at the pace of a five-minute mile, she lands with a force 3.2 times her body weight. That's a little above average. Distance runners with unusually high force measurements might be advised to switch to shoes with more cushioning or to change the way they land on their feet, to help prevent stress fractures or other leg injuries.

The Treadmill. The treadmill test offers another method of evaluating Gail's footwork. Runners generally land on their heels with a rolling motion that distributes the force of impact and prevents injuries to the feet, ankles, knees, and hips. To make sure Gail's feet are not rolling too much, technicians attach silver dots to her heels and lower legs that reflect light onto a camera behind the treadmill. The videotape is processed by a computer program that creates a connect-the-dot picture of her heel and ankle motion.

The treadmill test also measures the length of Gail's stride, one of the most important factors in running speed. A runner can increase her speed in two ways. She can take more steps per second until her muscles can contract no faster. Or she can increase her stride length, the distance from one right footprint to the next right footprint. But after a certain point, increasing stride length not only costs extra energy but actually slows a runner down. The leading leg can act like a brake if the foot gets too far ahead of the body.

Gail's treadmill test is recorded by a high-speed film camera that will provide a side view of her performance. The camera will be recording 200 images each second, faster than the eye can see. The film can be replayed in slow motion, allowing coaches and athletes to spot lapses in technique that they might otherwise overlook.

Film Digitization. The film of Gail on the treadmill will be analyzed later in the laboratory of biomechanist Keith Williams at the University of California at Davis. In a process called "digitizing," researchers will project the film, one frame at a time, on a "digitizer," a light table that acts like a piece of electronic graph paper. Using a cursor, they will mark the location of seven key spots on Gail's head, neck, trunk, and legs. The coordinates of each spot are relayed electronically to a computer. The technicians then advance the film to the next image and repeat the whole process.

From this information, the computer can create a series of animated stick figures, a kind of X-ray view of the athlete's running technique, and analyze factors like leg speed and knee lift that help determine performance.

In a process called "digitization," researchers analyze film of runners one frame at a time to create animated stick figures. These figures highlight factors like arm movement and trunk angle that can affect a runner's performance.

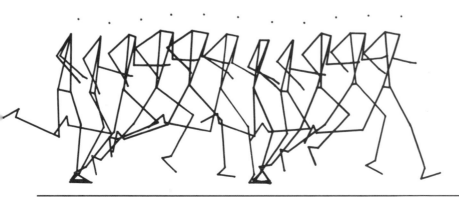

Backstroke Gets a New Kick

When twenty-one-year-old David Berkoff swam most of the first lap of the 100-meter backstroke underwater at the 1988 U.S. Olympic trials, he not only broke the world record. He also introduced a new technique that could permanently change the sport. He developed it by emulating another champion swimmer: the dolphin.

The dolphin powers its graceful leaps into the air by pumping its tail up and down in the water. Berkoff borrowed the dolphin kick, moving both legs together underwater, to maintain the thrust he achieved by pushing off the wall at the start of the race. He and his coach, Joe Bernal, determined that he would meet less resistance swimming underwater than at the surface, where he would make waves. Like the dolphin, he would dive deep – almost to the bottom of the pool – using a powerful upward kick to counteract the buoyant force of the water that was constantly pulling him up.

Exactly how long could the Harvard senior stay down before he would start to lose speed? On the advice of an expert in fluid dynamics, Berkoff decided to break through the water about thirty-two meters from the start, two-thirds the length of an Olympic-sized pool. This submarine-like maneuver has since been banned at international meets, but it garnered the swimmer Olympic silver in the individual 100-meter backstroke, and gold in the 4 x 100-meter medley relay.

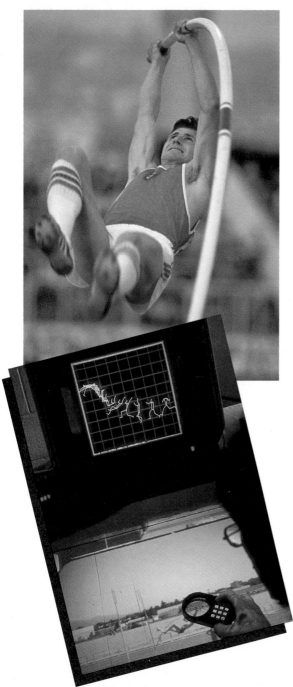

To date, Keith Williams has studied films of roughly fifty male and fifty female elite runners. He does not expect to identify a single ideal distance running style. One model would not fit the needs and body type of all runners any more than a single shoe style fits all runners, he explains. But some clues are emerging about what types of movement can help or hurt performance. On the whole, says Williams, the best distance runners have good flexibility that allows them to fully extend their legs when they push off the ground. They don't stand upright, but lean their trunks forward a small amount, about five degrees.

They also tend to avoid habits that waste energy and slow them down. They generally don't take strides that are too long, cross their feet in front of their bodies instead of planting them right beneath their hips, or bounce up and down too much.

Gail sailed through the biomechanical tests. The treadmill test showed that her stride length, about twelve feet two inches (3.70 m) for her five-foot eight-inch (1.72-m) frame, was longer than average for her height. But her oxygen uptake tests showed that the long stride was not wasting energy. "I don't think there was anything I would change," said Williams. The faster she ran, the more efficient she became – a sign that she is well-suited to middle- rather than long-distance running.

The oxygen uptake tests also helped U.S.O.C. consultants make detailed recommendations for her training. They determined exactly how fast she needed to run to boost her "VO_2 max," the maximum amount of oxygen she could deliver to her muscles.

"I thought it was helpful," said Gail after the camp. "I have a few things to work on mechanically. I have better guidelines on the

Soviet athlete Sergei Bubka (top) holds the world record in the pole vault. A researcher (bottom) uses a computer to analyze the position of a vaulter's joints at each stage of the vault.

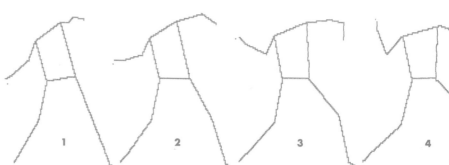

1   2   3   4

training times. When you put it all together – improving VO$_2$ max, increasing my anaerobic threshold – hopefully it will improve the bottom line."

The Limits of Human Performance

When the next Olympics rolls around in 1992, Gail will be thirty years old. Traditionally, people have thought middle-distance runners peaked in their mid-twenties. But, says Gail, "a lot of people get better as they mature. Francie Larrieu Smith, who was the United States' top performer at the 1988 Olympics in the 10,000-meter, was thirty-five years old." Her teammate Evelyn Ashford became the oldest sprinter to win an Olympic medal in the 100-meter at the age of thirty-one.

Athletes are accomplishing many other feats unthinkable a few decades ago. One reason is that they are training harder, and they are training year-round. Another factor, says physiologist

Roger Clemens' delivery is a chain reaction that starts in the leg and works its way up through the trunk and arm with the hand moving as quickly as the tip of a whip.

Pitching Mechanics

Pitching, says Dr. Arthur Pappas, medical director for the Boston Red Sox, is a total body activity. To better understand the contribution of each joint in the body and the punishment it must take, Pappas and team physical therapist Richard Zawacki used high-speed cinematography and computer processing to analyze the deliveries of twenty major league pitchers.

The stick-figure sequence below records an overarm fastball thrown by right-handed pitcher Roger Clemens, two-time winner of the Cy Young Award. The two-second pitch is divided into three stages: windup, acceleration, and follow-through.

During the first four frames, Clemens positions himself to deliver maximum force to the ball. Frame 5 shows him pushing off with his left foot. In an overarm throw, roughly half the velocity comes from the movement of the leg and trunk, and the other half from the arm. As the leg is planted, it sets up a chain reaction that works its way up through the legs to the hips, trunk, shoulder, elbow, and wrist. Each joint moves a little faster than the one before, with the hand snapping as quickly as the tip of a whip.

The acceleration phase (frames 7 through 9) starts with the shoulder fully extended to the back. It ends one-twentieth of a second later when the pitcher releases the ball at speeds ranging from eighty to a hundred miles per hour (130-160 km/h). The faster the shoulder moves, the more speed it gives to the ball. Braking this powerful shoulder action during follow-through is the job of the three small muscles in the back of the shoulder called the *rotator cuff*. The wear and tear makes the muscles waste away. Unless the pitcher rebuilds them with daily exercises, says Zawacki, he will start losing control over the ball.

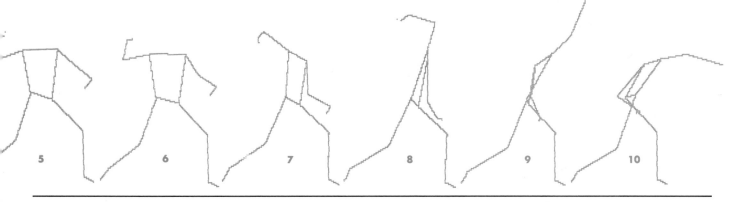

"'Roids"

At age twenty-one, Robb Fratus was a six-foot one-inch, 178-pound (1.85-m, 80-kg) kid who liked to hang out at the gym and pump iron. Five years later he had transformed himself into a 330-pound (150-kg) regional power-lifting champion who lived for his sport and could dead lift 750 pounds (340 kg) .

He might have added a national championship title to his name. But right before the competition he landed in the hospital with toxic hepatitis, liver damage caused by a drug or poison. He is convinced the secret of his success also caused his downfall: anabolic steroids.

Anabolic steroids are slightly altered, lab-made versions of the male sex hormone testosterone. The U.S. government recently banned their distribution for non-medical purposes. Once believed to be the domain of weight lifters, steroid use has spread through the world of sports and even into high schools.

Ben Johnson of Canada, the world's fastest sprinter, made headlines when he was stripped of his gold medal at the 1988 Summer Olympics after a urine test revealed signs of steroid use. But a few experts charged that at least half the athletes participating in the Seoul Games had used steroids in training. Some athletes are now turning to other substances that are more difficult to detect.

Anabolic steroids are believed to stimulate muscles to take in more protein when stressed, enabling users to make greater gains in muscle bulk and strength when they train intensely. The drugs also are believed to help athletes train harder by reducing fatigue and helping muscles recover faster after a workout. Finally, they seem to make users more aggressive.

What's wrong with using them? For one thing, says Charles Yesalis, a professor at Pennsylvania State University, the medical risks are still unclear. "I'm concerned we have a lot of kids using these drugs and no idea what will happen to them twenty years down the line."

Scientists do know that steroids can speed up the whole growth pattern, says Dr. Arthur Pappas. "The drugs can close down the growth centers in bones prematurely," he says. "The kids actually can end up smaller than they were destined to be."

Other health risks are less clear. Scientific studies have not been conducted using doses of steroids as massive as athletes are believed to take. Furthermore, effects seem to vary from one individual to the next. For adult men, reported side effects include liver damage, an increased risk of heart disease from high blood pressure and high cholesterol, and reduced production of sperm. These complications are believed to disappear if steroid use is stopped, but little is known about long-term use.

But stopping is no easy task, says Fratus. He took steroids in the recommended "cycles" – six to eight weeks of use, followed by several weeks of giving the body a rest. As time went on, his drug-free cycles became shorter and shorter until it was difficult to give up the steroids at all. "You've worked so hard to get to the point you're at that you don't want to backslide, and that's what happens when you go off steroids," he explains. He would look in the mirror and feel like his arms were shrinking before his very eyes.

There are ethical issues, as well. Taking steroids, says Dr. Pappas, is cheating, giving the user an unfair edge. Yesalis is concerned that if athletes feel they need to take steroids to compete, drug use will change the very nature of sports.

For Robb Fratus, steroids are part of a larger problem. "To me, the moral issue isn't steroids, it's our attitude about competition. People don't get a pat on the back for being number two or number three." He changed his priorities during the four weeks he was sick in bed. "Sports are games," he says. "They're not worth losing your health over."